I0814254

An Imprint of Pop!
popbooksonline.com

The Eras of Taylor Swift

THE FEARLESS era

Track List

1. Fearless
2. Fifteen
3. Love Story
4. Hey Stephen
5. White Horse
6. You Belong With Me
7. Breathe (ft. Colbie Caillat)
8. Tell Me Why
9. You're Not Sorry
10. The Way I Loved You
11. Forever & Always
12. The Best Day
13. Change

by Grace Hansen

This book is filled with videos, puzzles, games, and more! Scan the QR codes* while you read, or visit the website below to make this book pop.

popbooksonline.com/Fearless

abdobooks.com

Published by Pop!, a division of ABDO, PO Box 398166, Minneapolis, Minnesota 55439.

Printed in the United States of America, North Mankato, Minnesota.

082025
012026

Cover Photo: Alexandra Tarasova (BigArtLab); Shutterstock Images
Interior Photos: AP Images; Getty Images; Shutterstock
Editors: Elizabeth Andrews and Anna Schwartz
Series Designer: Laura Graphenteen

Library of Congress Control Number: 2025941212

Publisher's Cataloging-in-Publication Data

Names: Hansen, Grace, author.
Title: The Fearless era / by Grace Hansen
Description: Minneapolis, Minnesota : Pop!, 2026 | Series: The eras of Taylor Swift | Includes online resources and index
Identifiers: ISBN 9781098248697 (lib. bdg.) | ISBN 9781098249212 (ebook)
Subjects: LCSH: Swift, Taylor, 1989- --Juvenile literature. | Popular music--Juvenile literature. | Popular (Songs, etc.)--Juvenile literature. | Albums--Juvenile literature. | Concerts--Juvenile literature. | Mass media and music--Juvenile literature.
Classification: DDC 782.42164094--dc23

*Scanning QR codes requires a web-enabled smart device with a QR code reader app and a camera.

TABLE OF CONTENTS

CHAPTER 1

ROUND TWO!

After the release of Taylor Swift's **debut** album in 2006, she became the opening act for many other country artists. While on the road, Taylor found quiet places to write more songs. She wanted her next album to be even better than her first. It would not be an easy feat.

WATCH A VIDEO HERE!

Meet Taylor
Birthday: December 13, 1989
Star Sign: Sagittarius
Place of Birth: West Reading, PA
Favorite Number: 13
Favorite Color: Purple
Favorite Meal: Chicken tenders
and a chocolate shake
Meredith Grey
13
Benjamin Button
XOXO
Olivia
Benson
Taylor Swift

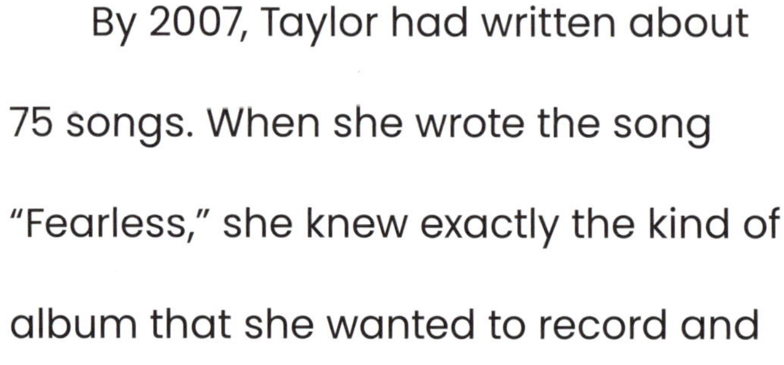

By 2007, Taylor had written about 75 songs. When she wrote the song "Fearless," she knew exactly the kind of album that she wanted to record and what to call it. When the touring finally came to an end, Taylor got back in the **studio**.

Taylor was just 18 years old when she released Fearless.

Taylor toured with country music legend George Strait in 2007.

But this studio was a little nicer than the last one she recorded in. “It had air conditioning,” Taylor would later joke. Taylor Swift was gaining fans and making waves in country music. Little did she know, *Fearless* would launch her into total **stardom**.

CHAPTER 2

COMPETING WITH HERSELF

Taylor was hopeful when she released *Fearless* on November 11, 2008. She had written 7 of the 13 tracks by herself and was a co-**producer** on the album. Like the album's name, Taylor said she had to be fearless to send more of her work out into the world. She also said she was only competing with herself. Taylor wanted *Fearless* to be even more popular than her **debut** album.

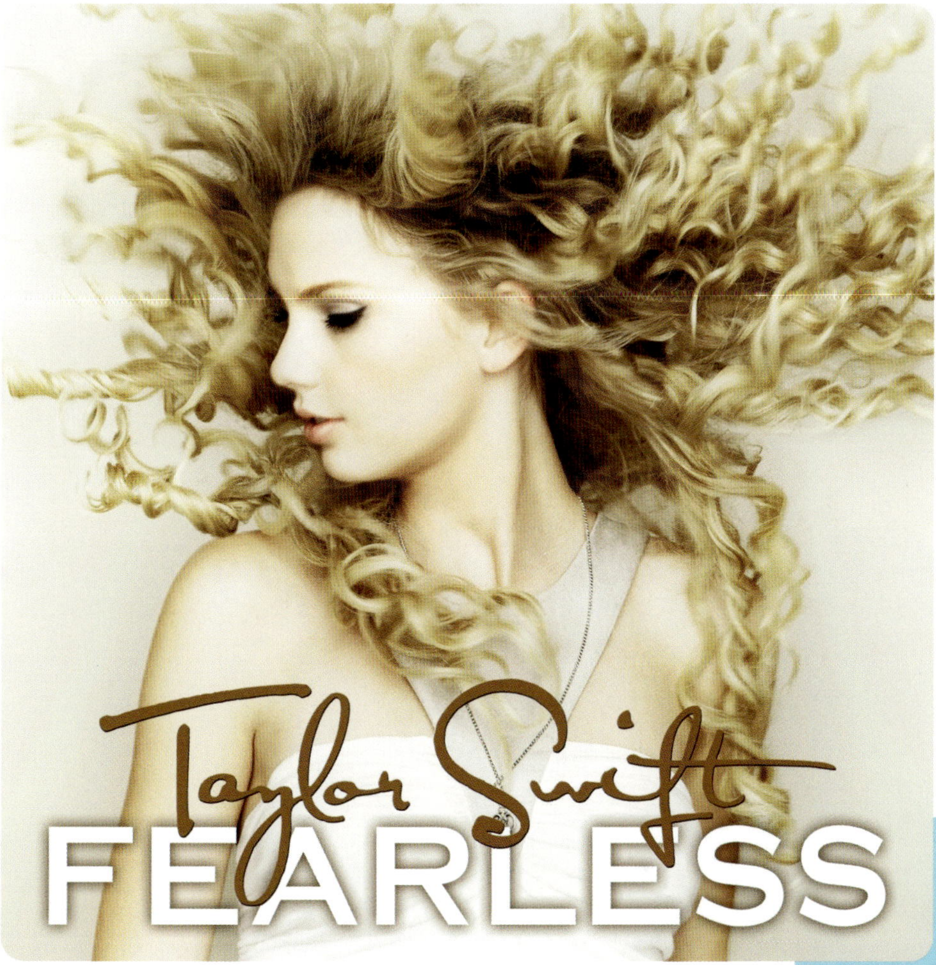

Taylor's wild, windblown hair gives the feeling of excitement and fearlessness.

EXPLORE LINKS HERE!

Taylor has often said that pop music icon Britney Spears inspired her.

Before the album's release, the **single** "Love Story" hit radio waves on September 15. Taylor said that the song completely changed her life. It also represents the album's recurring themes of young love, fairy tales, and coming of age.

Taylor said her songs are like diary entries. And she considers *Fearless* a collection of her diary entries from ages 16 to 18. When writing a diary, people share details about the things they go through and how they feel. Taylor was once unsure about writing songs with so many personal details. But she soon learned it created a connection with her fans because they could relate to her songs.

Taylor performed "Love Story" at the 42nd Annual CMA Awards.

Taylor's second album sold more than 3 million copies in its first year. It also made her an international star, topping charts throughout the world. *Fearless* became the most awarded country

Taylor couldn't hang on to all of her Grammy awards!

Taylor poses with Fearless co-producer Nathan Chapman.

album in history. And at the 52nd annual **Grammy Awards** in February 2010, it took home four awards, including Album of the Year. Taylor, just 20 years old, was the youngest artist to win Album of the Year at the time. *Fearless* did better than Taylor could have ever dreamed.

CHAPTER 3

BEHIND THE LYRICS

Taylor has said that she deals with her problems through songwriting. She also draws a lot of inspiration from her life and experiences when writing. The songs on *Fearless* are no different.

COMPLETE AN ACTIVITY HERE!

The marching band-inspired outfit is a nod to Taylor not fitting in with the so-called "popular kids" in school.

The Kanye West incident would kick off a yearslong feud between the artists.

Taylor recalled a time when she overheard a bandmate on the phone being yelled at by his girlfriend. She felt bad for him. As she walked away, she hummed and sang in her head, "You're on the phone with your girlfriend, she's upset." She quickly ran back to her tour bus and wrote out the first verse. The song would later become "You Belong With Me," one of the album's most popular songs.

HOT MIC MOMENT

In 2009, at the annual MTV Video Music Awards, Kanye West **infamously** stole the microphone away from Taylor while she accepted the Best Female Video award for her "You Belong With Me" music video. Kanye West told a shocked crowd that Beyoncé should have won the award.

Hidden Message

Taylor included hidden messages in the *Fearless* lyric booklet. The hidden message for "You Belong With Me" is "Love is blind, so you couldn't see me."

"Love Story" is a song that Taylor wrote in her bedroom. She drew inspiration from a boy she liked that her friends and family did not approve of. She likened it to the story of *Romeo and Juliet* by William Shakespeare. In Taylor's version of the story, Romeo and Juliet get married. She said it was the happily ever after that the characters deserved.

Taylor often wore Shakespeare-inspired dresses to perform "Love Story."

Several Taylor Swift songs are believed to be inspired by her past relationship with Joe Jonas.

Taylor wrote "White Horse" about the same boy that "Love Story" was inspired by. Unfortunately, this fairy tale did not have a happy ending. In the song, the narrator realizes that her boyfriend is not the Prince Charming she thought he was.

Taylor has said that she took inspiration from Brad Paisley's writing when she wrote songs for Fearless.

Taylor wrote "Fearless" in mid-2007 while on tour with country artist Brad Paisley. She was not dating anyone at the time. She said, "I think sometimes when you're writing love songs ... you write about what you wish you had. So, this

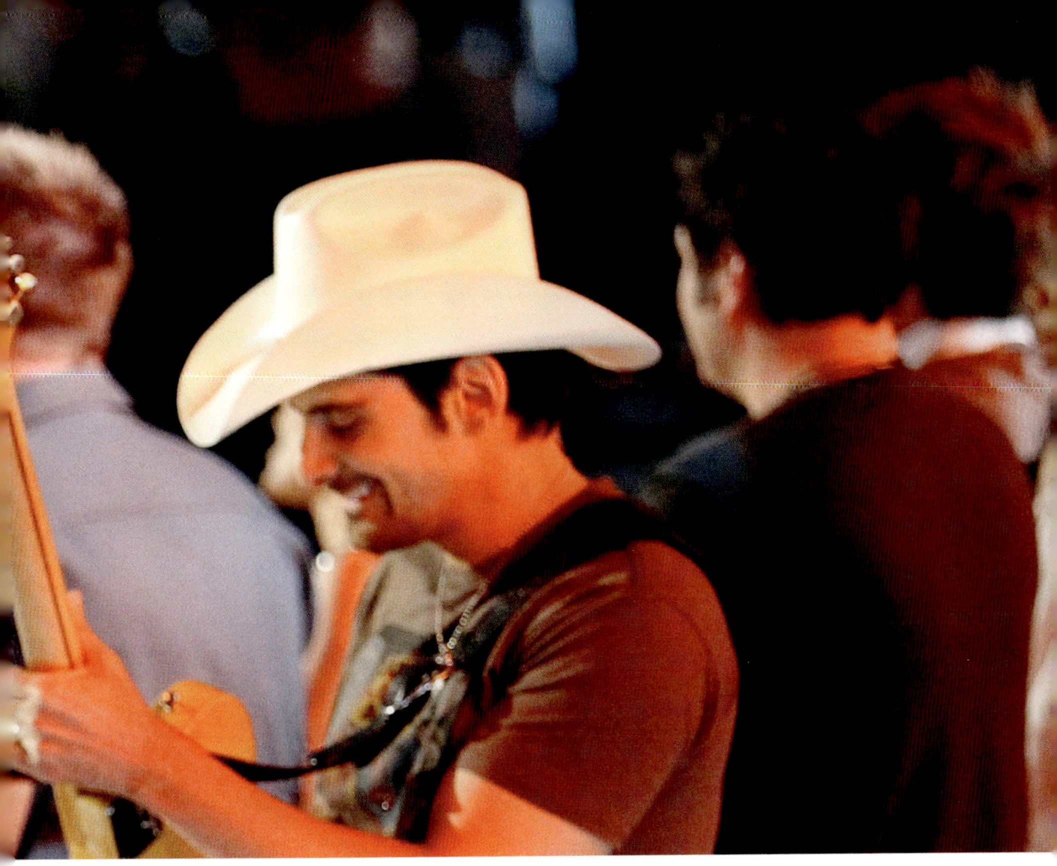

song is about the best first date I haven't had yet." Taylor said it was the type of song that she knew would be the album's title track as soon as she wrote it.

Hidden Message

The hidden message in the "Fearless" lyrics is "I loved you before I met you."

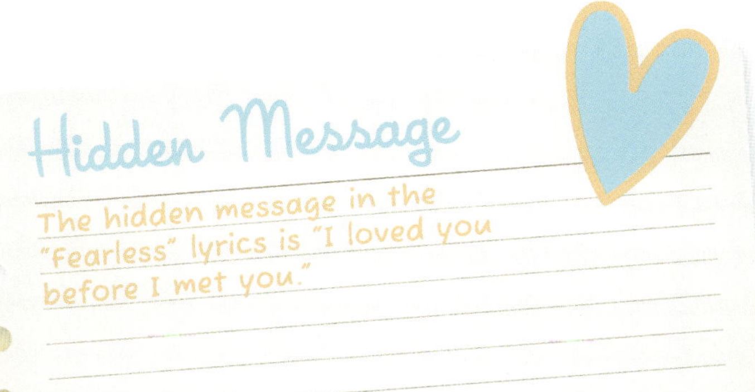

CHAPTER 4

LIVING FEARLESSLY

In January 2009, Taylor announced her first **headlining** tour! *Fearless* was hitting the road. Many shows sold out within minutes. The tour kicked off in Evansville, Indiana, on April 23. In the end, Taylor played 118 shows to more than 1 million fans.

LEARN MORE HERE!

Rhinestones and shimmering layers of fringe adorned most of Taylor's guitars and clothing throughout her Fearless *years.*

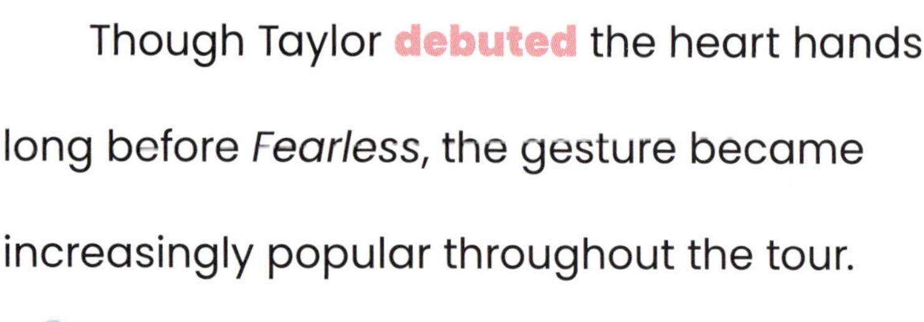

Though Taylor **debuted** the heart hands long before *Fearless*, the gesture became increasingly popular throughout the tour.

Taylor uses the heart hands to tell her fans "something between 'I love you' and 'Thank you.'" And fans mirror her to tell her the same.

No words are needed when Taylor and her fans put up the heart hands.

The *Fearless (Taylor's Version)* vinyl has 27 songs, including 6 unreleased songs.

On April 9, 2021, the long-anticipated *Fearless (Taylor's Version)* was released. It would be the first of many albums that Taylor would rerecord in the effort to own her music. The album was praised for its stronger vocals and **production** quality. Taylor said that the experience of rerecording *Fearless* was **sentimental**, since the album was so important to her growth as a person and songwriter. In the end, Taylor felt that the rerecorded version was even better than the original.

Beginning in 2023, *Fearless* would be featured again in the Eras Tour. Appropriately, Taylor made the *Fearless* Era her second act. To open it, a curtain of blinding gold rained down, illuminating an otherwise dark stage. The word FEARLESS appeared on the screen. The door opened to reveal Taylor with her guitar covered in silver rhinestones and the number 13. She skipped down the

Fans made and wore stacks of friendship bracelets to exchange at the Eras Tour concert.

The movement of Taylor's Eras Tour dress is similar to her hair on the Fearless *album cover.*

stage as she started to play "Fearless." The songs "You Belong With Me" and "Love Story" followed.

Some Eras Tour concertgoers wore outfits inspired by the Fearless Era.

Some fans thought that the *Fearless* Era was the best set of the show. Concertgoers described the energy that came with the era and noticed how loud the stadium got. They also loved that the band joined Taylor onstage for most of the set. Many recalled that *Fearless* is the album that officially made them Swifties.

The fringed Fearless *Era dress reminds fans to live fearlessly.*

MAKING CONNECTIONS

TEXT-TO-SELF

What is your favorite song from the *Fearless* Era? Why is it your favorite?

TEXT-TO-TEXT

Have you read books about any other music artists? How are they similar to or different from Taylor Swift?

TEXT-TO-WORLD

As a reader, why do you think so many people around the world connect with Taylor Swift and her music? Write a few sentences to explain your answer.

GLOSSARY

debut — to appear for the first time, or the first appearance.

Grammy Awards — an event that recognizes and awards remarkable works in music throughout the year.

headlining — being the main attraction.

infamously — in a way that is well known for some bad quality or deed.

producer — someone who organizes the creation of music recordings. Production is the act or process of producing.

sentimental — causing or showing tender feelings.

single — a song that is released as a stand-alone from the album.

stardom — the status of a star or celebrity.

studio — a place where recordings are made.

INDEX

This book is filled with videos, puzzles, games, and more! Scan the QR codes* while you read, or visit the website below to make this book pop.

popbooksonline.com/Fearless

*Scanning QR codes requires a web-enabled smart device with a QR code reader app and a camera.